MW00911678

ALL I NEED TO KNOW I LEARNED FROM THE GOLDEN GIRLS

OR: GROWING UP GOLDEN

T.A. PRYOR

Copyright © 2018 T. A. Pryor
All rights reserved.

Original Cover Design © 2018 by T.A. Pryor

All rights reserved.

The characters and events portrayed in this book are completely non-fictitious.
Any similarity to real persons, living or dead, or actual events is purely intentional and exactly what the author wanted to convey.

No part of this book may be reproduced, scanned, or stored in a retrieval system or distributed in any printed, recorded, or electronic form without permission. Please do not participate in or encourage piracy of copyrighted materials in violation of the author's rights. Purchase only authorized editions.
Piracy is for douches.

To Roo for always believing in me. To my parents for letting me watch t.v. as a kid. To the Brit for his unwavering support.
And to Betty White, Rue McClanahan, Estelle Getty, and Bea Arthur - thanks for the laughs.

Staying Golden

"Look, you didn't ask me for my opinion, but I'm old, so I'm giving it anyway." -Sophia

---

Lately I find myself wondering what those four sassy old broads in Florida would have made of today's political, moral, and cultural climate. I'm not really sure if anything is that far removed from life in the 1980s, but some days it feels as though everything has changed while at the same time nothing is different.

Perhaps it's that mass media, technology, and other innovations bombard us with information. It could be that we, as a nation, are living in a surreal alternate reality confused by the politics of partisanship. Or maybe it's just that somedays it feels like the world has lost its mind and is no longer safe. Not that it ever was safe, but one could argue that it may have felt that way for some. My mother for one makes that argument all the time and stands by her opinion that things were safer and simpler when she was a kid.

Picture it: Upstate New York, the 1950s. On a cold and snowy day a young girl is trudging uphill through the freezing snow lugging a case that contains her most treasured possession- her bowling ball. I'm sure all of our parents have that, "You think your life is hard…" story that is bursting with some kind of drudgery that they themselves endured so we could be grateful that life has improved due to their sacrifices. My mom's version had a bowling ball. Oh, and she lived in a berg replete with ice storms so severe that the entire town would (and I think still does) shut down for a week.

Mom laments quite often of wishing she could be back there in her teeny, tiny, frigid, hazardous-to-your-health-because-a-falling-icicle-could-kill-you home-town. When this happens I usually just stare at her quizzically and wonder why on earth she would want to do that. But back to the kinder, gentler, America.

My mother regularly points to her childhood as proof that the world today is far more dangerous. When she was younger, "nobody" locked their doors at night. Children ran rampant through their neighborhoods audaciously accepting candy from strangers, and women could walk around most parts of town without the clear and present danger of molestation, ogling, or any other harassment.

To be fair, when put on the spot as to the notion of there being *no* crime when she was growing up, my mom did have to admit that there was a scandalous three person homicide when she was in high school. Oh, and she seemed to remember it had to do with a drug deal gone south, and maybe a gang. Also, one of her relatives may have been a suspect. But I digress…

So, if the 1950s were as innocent and childlike as my mother describes then the 1980s must have seemed like a bloodbath in comparison. In fact, in a report by Radford College there were more serial killers on the prowl in the 1980s than any of the decades before it or since.

It's a miracle we made it out alive. The "me decade" was full of killers. Not to mention there was also a Cold War raging, terrorists hijacking planes, the Challenger exploded, Reagan was shot, John Lennon was assassinated, Madonna writhed on stage at the inaugural MTV Video Awards (it's possible she's still doing that), it was a mess.

The U.S. alone had foreign debts, homeless Vets, AIDs, Crack, Bernie Goetz... and while we didn't start the fire (Billy Joel did) we were having a hell of time trying to put it out. Yet, for all of its violence the 80s were also the era birthed by the efforts of the feminists from the 60s and 70s.

Films such as *Working Girl* and *Baby Boom* showed us women in the rat race as more than secretaries. In *Baby Boom* the protagonist was a woman who was not determined to be defined by motherhood (well, initially anyway).

Meanwhile, over on television, *Designing Women* and *Murphy Brown* featured female characters who were intelligent and opinionated while at the same time forceful, fearless, and no nonsense. More importantly, they were flawed.

The typical female stereotype on t.v. had most often been women like Carol Brady, June Cleaver, and Miriam Cunningham or rather the embodiment of the idea of the middle class white woman who was happy to stay at home and raise her children, feed her family, and do the housework. These boilerplate "moms" were great in that this particular archetype frequently makes us, the viewer, feel good. However, they really are not representative of real women.

Real women are crazy flawed, trust me, I know. Television today does a much better job at illustrating this point and there is a plethora of shows that strive to bring us different types of feminine attributes presented in an assortment of situations. Yet, in the early 1980s, complex, personality rich, flawed women were not yet readily available to us.

We did have Maude, Florida Evans, Louise Jefferson, and Mary Richards and while they were mouthier, more opinionated, and more substantial embodiments of real women they were still not quite the neurotic messes most of us feel like. Then, in 1985 a change came, or rather a show came about that presented to the audience not one, but four very real women collectively known as *The Golden Girls*. They were funny, they were flawed, and they were fabulous.

What made the *Golden Girl's*, or the GG's as my husband calls them, so relatable was that they were similar to ourselves and the women we knew. What made them awesome was that they looked like our grandmothers.

The show's creators didn't just bring to life four sassy women making it work from day to day. They made these sassy women much closer to the grave than the cradle. This is the inherent brilliance of the show: by creating characters who were sixty and not twenty it made their shenanigans and issues framable in a manner that said, "Oh, well if it's okay for my grandma to like or do that, then maybe it's okay for me too." It also said, "Holy crap! My grandma is doing THAT!?" This concept was unheard of on television prior to the show, and since it went off the air in 1992 there have been any number of attempts to capture the magic that these four characters made together. And characters they were…

Blanche wantonly hustled after men and was neither ashamed nor abashed by her sexual conduct. She was like a one woman frat house, intent on getting laid above all else.

Dorothy was smart and reveled in that fact, but she also had gambling issues, anxiety, and terrible taste in men. Rose was naive, but she also saved the day on many an occasion and battled with real problems such as being exposed to HIV. Sophia was cantankerous, sassy, and everything I wanted to be as an octogenarian. She didn't let anyone get in her way, including her own daughter.

They laughed, they cried, they caroused and in the end what these characters taught us and continue to teach us is that there are a few basic tenets for a good life: do the right thing, ALWAYS. Keep an awesome network of family and friends and when times get tough prepare yourself with forgiveness at the ready. Relationships are really hard. Fight aging with everything you got (not just your own aging, but aging in others too). If you're prejudiced or bias, get over yourself and while you're at it, overcome your fears too. Let go and move forward when you have to, but respect yourself and treasure your growth along the way.

Lastly, and most importantly, always keep reaching for your dreams no matter how old you are, no matter what hurdles get in the way, especially if the biggest hurdle is yourself.

On Love

Rose: Tell me, is it possible to love two men at the same time.

Blanche: Set the scene, have we been drinking?

In between getting divorced from husband number one (the Canadian), and marrying husband number two (The Brit), I went on a lot of dates. That old saying that "you have to kiss a lot of toads before you find your prince" is nowhere near correct. It's more like you have to dodge the red-hot pelvic thrusts of many a crap-weasel before you find someone willing to tolerate you and your particular brand of maniac. And by maniac, I mean baggage.

It begs the question: is it possible for us to leave our baggage behind. Better question: why would we? For better or worse our baggage is part of what makes us who we are. Out of our hurts, scars, and failings comes our steeliness and fortitude. We might also get a little fearful, unable to trust, reluctant to love again, bitter, and resentful, but those are also part of who we are.

Thus, I think it is fair to say that the fairytales got it all wrong — we don't need a prince to sweep us off our feet. What we need is a kind, tolerant, strapping hunk of a man capable of lifting our baggage and hauling it wherever we go. Tolerant and hunk being key.

When I think about my own baggage I realize that

while some people's emotional baggage is equal to a carry-on, mine is more in the vicinity of the several trunks the Howell's managed to take with them to *Gilligan's Island*. Why did they have those trunks? It was a three hour tour! It actually makes less sense than Ginger wearing stoles on the island.

Speaking of crap weasels and baggage - when I married my first husband my mother tried to warn me, "Never marry a Canadian! Their bacon is ham with an identity crisis and maple syrup is a bitch to clean up." It's possible she didn't say that, but it's a good adage to live by just the same. Years after my divorce it's also still easier to remember my mom warning me about bacon than what she really said which had something to do with us not being right for each other.

To be fair, we *weren't* right for each other. He was much more compatible with the woman with whom he cheated on me. They got married like a month after our divorce and as far as I know they've lived happily ever after.

I wasn't as smart as the ex in that I didn't have a new mate built into my first marriage. I hear that doing so is quite convenient. Consequently, after we got divorced I went on scores of dates with some real interesting characters (that's putting it mildly). Maybe it wasn't scores of dates, more like a dozen. And it wasn't right after the divorce as much as it was three years after plus another three years of avoiding authentic relationships. So, like six years after the divorce I went on a handful of dates. Horrible, soul crushing, morality questioning dates. Whoever says that dating is fun is lying. Or a masochist. Or both.

The GG's had what can only be described as a

plethora of dates. Blanche accounted for the majority, but the others were no slouches. Dorothy got picked on by the others for her dry spells but she still had more dates per capita than most of us. Sophia kept her hand in with a few boyfriends here and there (I think they were all named Tony) and Rose had at least a dozen short term boyfriends prior to meeting her steady beau, Miles Weber.

Rose actually dated Miles back in season one when his name was Arnie - neither of them mentioned that three years later when they met again. Side note - Miles was in witness protection and his real name was Nicholas Carbone. Later, we find out he was on the lam in Amish country as Samuel Plankmaker. Thus, maybe instead of Arnie being another plot inconsistency he was one of Miles' alter egos. We could argue that Rose would have known, but I think we all know that's not necessarily true.

So, like the GG's, I had my share of interesting dates. Dating now doesn't seem like it was back in their day. On t.v. and in movies there is always the meet-cute where the main characters have this adorable encounter out there in the real world. It absolutely does not work this way in real life.

These days if you go to a bar with your wingman you find the over forty set looking for their youth, the over sixty set looking to score with a youth, and the under thirty set with their douchy hats and Snidley Whiplash mustaches. Actually that's not fair - not all of them wear a hat. Long story short - or shorter - my sister convinced me that I needed to go the online dating route.

First, she conned me into E-Harmony. I spent hours

jumping through all of their hoops and filling out all of their questionnaires only to be told that they didn't have anyone compatible with me for sixty miles. Sixty miles!?! That meant that nobody who had signed up for that service within a large populated area of California would find my brand of kooky delightful.

The site told me to wait a day or two, matches were on the way. I waited a week and opened up my options to the entire state. Nothing. It wasn't the least bit soul sucking either (insert deep sigh and eye roll here). Rather then wait around for a match to be found I ditched the E-Harm and joined a few of the other sites - two paid for and one that was free. Subsequently, like the Girls, I had a few dates with some rather interesting (or dubious) characters.

To me, Rose had the most interesting dating life. With the exception of Dick Van Dyke and Leslie Nielsen, Dorothy seemed to date a lot schmucks (and that's not counting Stan). Sophia had the aforementioned Tony's and Blanche went through a slew of men but never seemed to keep the particularly good ones. The key to Rose perhaps, was that on the whole she was far more accepting of people's flaws than her roommates. She wasn't searching for an Adonis or someone with money, rather just someone nice with whom she could spend time. Maybe this was due to her naivety or small town ideas or maybe she was just more open minded than the others. However you slice it she was far more apt to date someone who was unconventional than her friends were.

For example: there was Dr. Jonathan Newman. He was a giant in the field of psychiatry and in stature he was a little person. Blanche couldn't keep her foot out of her mouth upon meeting him whereas Rose not only dated him, she pictured herself marrying him and overcoming the adversities that may be put upon their relationship due to his height limitations. In the end that relationship didn't work out, but it was due to Rose not being Jewish rather than Jonathan not being taller. Go figure.

As the years went by Rose dated a man who thought he was a superhero, a man with impotency issues (she helped him overcome them - talk about a patient woman!), and a con artist after Charlie's pension. At one point she was even haplessly semi-dating a lesbian (unbeknownst to her). When she found out that her new gal pal was in love with her she was kind enough to explain that had she too been gay she would be proud to have such a person as her love. And that kindness was essentially the root of Rose's character. Betty White deserved every award and accolade she received for playing Rose as she was able to take the archetypal dumb blonde and elevate her to a position where she was truly the heart and soul of the show.

It is easy to mistake Roses' naivety for stupidity or to think less of her because she wasn't an academic. That would be missing the point of the character which is: she was symbolic of a universal and forgiving love. She loved not with her eyes or mind but with her heart which allowed for her to see in others what the shallow care not to see.

As a single lady I was inspired by Rose and believed I should date without being judgmental and care for others based on who they were on the inside. Suffice it to say, that is a dating approach that works best only for Rose Nylund.

Over the short time that I was drowning in the dating pool I went on a date with a guy who halfway through the meal felt that in the interest of all honesty he should tell me that he had been in prison... like recently been in prison. Like had been released six weeks prior to the date been in prison. I may have slept with him, but in my defense he dropped the soap in the shower so I was compelled by societal convention to do it.

On another date I had appetizers with a guy who then took me to help him pick out new work shoes. I didn't sleep with him - his taste in shoes was dreadful.

After those two and pre-Brit I was matched with (but didn't meet in person) a very flashy photographer who thought the way to a woman's heart was through his penis.

We hadn't spoke on the phone or met in person. We had just chatted in that wonderful realm of anonymity that is the internet. Part way through our IM conversation about something as mundane as what we had eaten for lunch, he decided what I really needed was a picture of his genitals.... in his hand... at full mast.

I laughed at his audacity for several minutes before I messaged him and advised that I didn't need to see his junk. I then went on to explain to him that for women seeing the male genitalia didn't usually have the same effect as female genitalia on view had for men. And, in the middle of my diatribe about how for the female sexuality was more of a combination of things like eyes, sense of humor, kindness, etc. he sent me another picture of his naughty bits. So I wished him luck and promptly closed that instant messenger account.

Following that debacle there was a sadist who I told I had Hep C and a chef with no driver's license who got me a speeding ticket, but those are stories for another day.

On Self-Acceptance

"Except for the fact that I've only made love in one position, I've led a very full life." - Sophia

---

When I married the Brit I chose a dress that didn't have sleeves. Initially, I planned to wear a shawl that covered my batwing upper arms… maybe not batwing, that implies a smaller size then they are. Hold on, I'll try again…

Initially, I planned to wear a shawl that covered my Boeing 747 upper arms. While we were dress shopping my sister had suggested that I consider wearing a jacket or bridal bolero with it. She wasn't being mean, she knew that most of my adult life I've had an ongoing war waged against my blubbery arms.

My mom, who was sitting alongside my sister that day, said one of the wisest things I've ever heard: "Wear what is comfortable. I don't know why you care about your arms. They're your arms. Who cares what anyone else might think?" So, I bought the thin, pretty shawl, wore it through the ceremony and took it off for the pictures.

Now I rebelliously wear short sleeved shirts in public like a bad-ass and I feel good about it. I walk down the street with my head held high and in my mind the opening riffs to "Stayin' Alive" are playing as I nod to people with a, "That's right, I'm awesome," look on my face. The people usually look back at me like, "That fat lady has something wrong with her... she might be demented." I'm okay with that though.

Of course the war I was previously fighting with my arms has now spread to every other part of my body. And, at some point you just kind of accept the fact that for now you're fat and there is no real hiding it. A paunchy stomach you misdirect from with a flowy shirt. With a serious gut, a huge sized booty and tree-trunk legs even a mumu says, "Make room people, I'm coming through!"

Like a lot of others, my adulthood has been spent in one endless, brutal, winner-take-all, prizefight with my size. I blame my mother. If she hadn't cooked delicious comfort food like her spaghetti or homemade mac n cheese maybe I wouldn't like food so much. Truly, this is her fault.

If she had fed me wheatgrass and edamame instead of goulash, I could be a size zero today. My father is culpable too. The man makes the most amazing country gravy with fried chicken remnants. I'm salivating a little just typing about it. I wonder if he's home tonight and what they're making for dinner.

I'm actually a pretty decent cook myself. Not to brag, but the kitchen is the one place I can frequently nail it. The problem being that I cook so well and everything is so delicious when it touches your lips, you naturally want more of it. I have had to be quite clever with avoiding second helpings of the meals I make. I do this by just having one massive helping the first go round.

A few years ago I taught a Citizenship class. Given that I'm married to a British expat and it was time for him to get his American citizenship I talked him into coming to the class. It was fantastic having him there as the butt of all my Revolutionary War jokes. I cracked myself up mocking his country's inability to take out some farmers with pitchforks.

Most of my class didn't speak English very well so they were no where near as amused with me as I was with myself. Anyway, when the Brit first came to class I advised the students he was my husband and to feel free to mock him for being English. A few of them missed the part about him being my spouse and over the course of the semester as they realized that he and I are married they were somewhat incredulous that he and I *could* be married.

Being a fair minded, self-loving individual my immediate thought is, "Why can't you believe it? Is it because he's Jack Sprat who could eat no fat and his wife could eat no lean?" I don't say this to them of course, but I think it and then I go home and grumble to myself over a donut.

For some of us our self-identity and by association self-worth is often tied up in those failings that most bother us. For Rose Nylund a lot of her self image rested in who she really was. Rose was the type of character who was always a chipper chicken and was seemingly free of self-doubt, self-effacement, and self-pity. That is until we learn that she was adopted and had spent her entire life living with the day dream that her biological father was Bob Hope. She knew in her heart that he wasn't really her father, but something in her loved something about him so much she held onto the childhood notion that he could be.

I think a lot of us secretly wonder who it is that we truly are. For example: am I really a middle aged, twice married (neither time to an American), former social-worker who now teaches Adult School part time? And if I am, then what the heck does that mean? Honestly? It means nothing.

Seriously - it means absolutely nothing because who I am has nothing to do with where I work or how I look. That's actually probably a good thing because I can't remember the last time I put on make-up since allergy season arrived and I've been baring my natural face, funny spots, red cheeks and all to the world. The other day a student asked me if I've been sick. I replied, "Is it because I'm not wearing make-up?" Chagrinned he admitted that was indeed the case. I think I told him to zip it or face a failing grade.

I feel like it's probably safe to say that a greater portion of the population do not do what they love for a living. The Brit does and my sister does, but outside of them and maybe a few other people I know everyone else just works to make money so that they can do or have whatever it is they want. Therefore, what we do can't possibly be entangled in who we are.

I'm sure that very few tombstones have, "Bob Smith, retired from the phone company after climbing poles for thirty years" on them. Instead, most tombstones read, "Loving wife," "Loving Brother" or something along those lines. I also question the idea that our titles define us. I am a sister, a wife, an ex-wife, a daughter, a niece, a co-worker, and a friend. But being a sister doesn't make who I am, *having* a sister does. As far as relationships go, outside of the one with my parents and my marriage, the one with my sister has been the most important in my life.

My other roles in life have been important too, but

maybe not as defining as sister-hood. This is due in part to her having suffered the same hostage situation as I did. Given we have shared childhood experiences she is the only other person on the planet that when I talk about my mom being crazy, she gets it. To be fair, all of us probably think our mother is crazy and to be honest, they are. But, they each have their own particular crazy which is most often something that they consistently say or do that only their children understand. Thus, my sister understands completely when I call her and skip the salutations to say, "Your mother!"

My sister and I are actually in all probability crazier than our mom and over the years have had many, many MANY fights. We have often relished getting the other one in trouble with the units (our parents) and we have sometimes gone out of our way to throw the other one under the bus (never with anything that would give either of the units a heart attack from shock, rather just your run of the mill misdeeds).

The worst was when my sister told our staunchly conservative Republican father that I had registered as an Independent. I remember it happened at dinner one night and as the words went from her lips to his ears we all watched in horror as his fork fell in slo-mo from his hand onto his plate. I think it was three weeks after before he could speak to me again and I'm pretty certain I caught the glimpse of a tear in the corner of his eye upon hearing the news. Alas, turnabout is fair play, and four years later my sister turned eighteen and registered as an Independent as well. Dad didn't drop his fork when I told him (again over dinner) about her, he just sighed deeply and gave my sister that, "Et tu Brutei?" glance.

All harassment aside, part of who I am is because I have a sister. She played a role in helping to shape the person I have become. Mostly through harassment, cajoling, name-calling, tattling, and slapping. Even today she constantly is on me to do better, to be better. It's actually pretty annoying.

When I used to smoke she would hound me all the time about quitting, going so far as to tell me how she will have to put my urn on her mantle so she can continue to lecture me after I've died of lung cancer. Being the stubborn older sibling I would refuse to listen to her but in the end I quit and I'll begrudgingly give her the victory. In retrospect my mom was pretty good with the guilt too. After she accidentally discovered that I smoked… she was supposed to be on her way to Utah but nooooooooo… she forgot her bowling ball at home and had my dad bring her back for it. How was I to know she was going to round the corner of our front walkway as I sat outside like a super cool teen smoking and talking on the phone to my bff?

So my sister… when I'm a jerk, and this happens more often than not, she's the one who calls shenanigans and implores me to at least attempt to be a better human being. When I do behave it's really only because I don't want to hear her lecture me again. In fact, most of my decisions are based on how willing I am to listen to her (or really anyone who might pay me lip service) should she find out what I did.

As for Rose, she did come to terms with the fact that Bob Hope was definitely not her biological father. Turns out it was Don Ameche. For those of you who don't know who Don Ameche is I refer you imdb.com and/or the fantastic old movie, *Moon Over Miami.*

Upon Rose eventually meeting her bio dad, Don Ameche, who incidentally was a monk, Rose was able to realize that she had had a great life in spite of not knowing him. She knew who she was, she was Rose Nylund - an orphan adopted into an awesome family who had a great childhood, an awesome marriage, good kids, and a pretty great life.

The moral to the story? It's not our biology, our jobs, or our facades that define us. It's those lifelong relationships with people who were trapped in the same hostage situation that do.

Our Parents, Ourselves

*Sophia [to Blanche]: Fasten your seat belt, slut puppy!...
This ain't gonna be no cakewalk!*

Relationships with our (parental) units are tricky. When we're kids we have to follow their rules (I don't know about yours, but mine had a lot and it took forever to break all of them). As young adults we set out into the unknown only to find that everything they had said over the years was true and they did know what they were talking about. Knowing that they were right about most things is particularly annoying, but that may just be me.

Later in life we wake up one day and find that are units are no longer spring chickens and our parents getting older seems to come with its own unique set of challenges. To their credit, my mother and father are both aging pretty well. At seventy-one they are both still active, they both still work, and most of the time they seem to still have all of their faculties.

A few months back the doctor told my mother that there was no reason why she couldn't make it to a hundred. My mother is skeptical about this, but I'm pretty sure she's got it in it her. I'm less certain my father will make it that long, not because of his health, but rather because one of these days mom might snap and put an end to him.

As a whole my dad is a pretty adorable old guy. He tootles around with his bestie several days a week pretending to be hard at work and he's a legend in his own mind down at the Elk's Lodge.

However, the older he gets the crankier he gets. This isn't good given the fuse for his patience is getting shorter each year. I never thought that fuse was very long to begin with. So, what was maybe a two inch fuse has probably been whittled down to less than an inch.

It doesn't help that he and my mother both have fiery personalities. Anyone who has spent any amount of time with the two of them at their kitchen table can attest that their sudden outbursts toward one another are a little jarring (to put it mildly).

My sister and I are used to it and are generally unphased. Most of the time we don't even really notice when they bicker. Non-veterans of the "flare-ups" are often terrified at first and will turn to my sister or I with a withering look that implores us to do something before someone winds up dead. They're probably horrified that we just continue to eat our meal but we know the most important rule of Parental Unit Fight Club: don't interupt Parental Unit Fight Club. Ever. If you do, people could die.

I told my parents once that I wanted to have little dolls made of them so that someday when they're gone I can reenact their greatest hits. One of my favorites is The Christmas Morning Egg Debacle:

Judy (non-aggressively): Mark, did you cook that egg in oil? You should have used butter.

Mark (LOUDLY): Goddamn it Judy! Do you want to make breakfast next time?

Judy (loud and exasperated): Oh Timothy Mark! Settle down!

Mark (under his breath): She's talking to me like it's the first time I've ever cooked before (he makes eye contact, you look away quickly or suffer the consequences). She should cook if she doesn't like it.

Judy (in a half mumble): I'm just saying, you don't cook eggs in oil. I've never seen anyone cook eggs in oil before. (in a whisper to you) Now the egg is greasy.

At this point my father will either go on like nothing happened or start round two. The crazy part, however, is not that there can be multiple rounds, but that each lasts under a minute and afterwards the two of them are totally cool with one another. If anyone is in trouble after a spat it's you if you were dumb enough to speak up, make eye contact, or pick a side. In fairness, you were warned.

Some people having witnessed these conversations between my parents are astonished that they're not divorced. I think its key to their near half century together. These two squabblers genuinely dig each other! After all these years and all those flare ups they are as in love now as they ever were. It's mind-blowing, sick, and cute all at the same time.

Being married to an Englishman, I find that such behavior doesn't work in our house. The first time I raised my voice at the Brit he stood still like petrified wood and stared at me, just blinking. I'm not even sure he was breathing. When I was done he looked as though I had skinned his puppy before he strode off gallantly with his head held high saying nary a word to me. I found myself seeking to apologize, feeling like a heel for being mean to such a sweet and noble creature. He quickly forgave me and it was two days later before I even realized what had happened.

For years I was caught up in this process where the Brit stepped in it, I "had a go at him" (his words), he did the stoic pout, and I apologized for being a terrible human being. At some juncture in this vicious cycle I had an epiphany as to what was happening and realized that he was soooooo clever.

I had foolishly prided myself on my ability to manipulate him while I was merely a pawn in his sick game of *Punk the Wife, Get Out of Trouble.* Now I just give him, "the look" which conveys that he's in a vat of scalding hot water and should he not reverse the situation or his actions he might be brutally murdered. The look has come to be the most powerful tool in my marriage arsenal. So I try to use it sparingly so as to not let him get used to seeing it.

I'm wondering if "the look" would ever work on my dad. I've seen my mom give him tons of looks over the years, none of which have seemed to stop him in his tracks. This is a little un-nerving given she has one look in particular that is so fierce it could topple governments. I think she reserves that one for me.

At their home Dorothy is the keeper of the looks for the GG's. As an actress, Bea Arthur was capable of conveying everything the audience needed to know with but a withering glance or facial gesture. She used her abilities well while doing the show especially when it came to scenes involving her and Estelle Getty's Sophia.

As previously noted, Sophia was a character who defied aging. She was determined to keep living with as much gusto as she could muster and always to the chagrin of her daughter. For example: When Sophia wanted to stay out all night carousing with the senior citizen set at Roofy's (I think it was a bar, not sure how they spelled it) Dorothy forbade her and Sophia chose to move out and live on her own terms.

As a driver Sophia was a menace to society, yet when Dorothy attempted to take her keys away Sophia just got around it by taking her roommates' cars. That was kind of the essence of Sophia's playbook - when Dorothy said no she went around her by using Blanche and Rose. Rose in particular was the usual victim of Sophia's ploys and often found that she had given Sophia money or recourses that Dorothy had previously denied.

I like to think that my parents will continue to age gracefully and defiantly like Sophia. I may have to parent them, or think I am parenting them, but they'll continue to be head strong and sassy. Sophia's in your face dissent from Dorothy's wishes is how I want my units to be when they're her age. Admittedly, I relish the idea of being the one who tells them what they can or can't do, turnabout is fair play. Yet, I equally relish them telling me off and living their lives on their terms.

Parenting

"[to Dorothy] Come here. Sometimes a mother gets a little busy and forgets to tell her daughter everything she needs to know. So I'm telling you now. Don't date a priest, it's bad luck. Trust me on this one." Sophia

---

Unless you count too many cats, two box turtles, a Brit, and an unruly old Basset Hound my parenting experiences are limited to men and pets. Sometimes the two haven't been mutually exclusive. If parenting a child is anything like trying to herd the aforementioned Basset Hound into behaving and being a productive citizen in society, I'm not sure I'm cut out for it; the dog is exhausting and causes a great amount of mental anguish. I couldn't imagine mini humans being any less so.

This hound dog who plagues me is actually not mine alone. He also belongs to my sister who was living with me following the end of my first marriage and prior to the start of her first one. Yeah, we both have been married twice. My parents who have been together for forty-seven years are so proud.

So, when Quincy the Basset Hound first arrived in our lives (via our aunt who used to breed Bassets) it was on a sunny Easter Sunday and before us was not one litter of odiferous, rollie-pollie Basset puppies, but two. They were enclosed in this cute little makeshift play-pen and there was some ungodly number of them, like, fourteen or fifteen.

My sister had always wanted a Basset Hound - one she could name Melvin and pull along in a Radio Flyer. I tried to have no part of what I felt was going to be a travesty: I already had 2 large mongrels and four cats at home (these are different cats than the ones previously mentioned) and I was determined to hold fast to my definitive "no" on the puppy. I was unyielding for all of 30 seconds.

Being as that we were dealing with puppies, and a boatload of them at that, over a dozen little noses were sniffing at us through their enclosure while tails wagged and puppy whines beseeched the air. If you have never seen a Basset Hound puppy you should know that they are the cutest of all puppies bar none. Sure, others puppies are adorable, but with those round bellies, big paws, short stature, and super awesome long ears, Bassets have that little something extra that other breeds are missing. Namely, they all smell like corn meal. I don't know how or why, but they do. All Bassets smell like corn meal… and trash. And a little like death.

Anyway, we spent forever scratching this guy and petting another, going the rounds to give them each a chance when suddenly - **HE** appeared. Atop of the other dogs leapt the fattest, most cuddly, and most captivating pile of odor I've ever smelt. His eyes locked with ours and it was love at first squeal, ours, not his.

Quickly, he body surfed over his siblings and cousins and you could tell he would have been there sooner if he hadn't been napping in the food bowl. He tripped over his long ears a couple of times, but still, he persisted until he was able to take two good leaps and pounce, face first, right into the side of pen. With haste we snatched him up and declared him the love our lives and quickly christened him, Quincy Melvin Satchel Howard Taft III. Then and there we took him home and so began the single greatest night of hell I or my sister had experienced up to that point in our lives.

He was too small to let run amok in the house, and he wasn't potty trained. The big dogs I already had weren't sure what they thought of him and my Rottweiler looked as though she figured he would make a great snack. To be safe, we put him in the bathroom for the night and from there he whined, he scratched at the door, he howled, he barked, he relieved himself on the floor (and not on the puppy pad provided), and he really went out of his way to ensure that nobody in the neighborhood was sleeping that night.

At work the next day I was trying to hook up an i.v. line for a caffeine drip when I received an email from my sister stating that we needed to take Quincy Melvin Satchel Howard Taft III back to our aunt.

My brain, bloodshot eyes, and langover (that's a hangover from lack of sleep) agreed, yet I somehow managed to tell her no. I gave her some lecture on how she wouldn't be able to send a crying human baby back when she had one therefore she needed to figure out how to parent her little bundle of misery.

She didn't really argue in return, she must have been too tired. This was a little shocking to me as arguing with me is her forte. I didn't hear from her again for hours and that night when she came home with a baby gate for our kitchen, a ginormous crate, a stuffed bear, and a dog bed I was more than a little perplexed. Deep down though, I was very impressed.

She was determined that she was going to thwart

the monster we had adopted and turn him into a delightful animal. It's occurring to me as I write this that's probably how my mother felt when I was a child. Maybe that's how every parent feels?

Blanche admitted to her friends that as a young mother she left her kids in the care of nannies citing her own selfishness as motivation for doing so. She wanted to be young, social, and carefree, not stuck at home being a mother. Subsequently, all six of her children, and especially her daughters, Janet and Rebecca, had significant resentment toward her.

Janet's mother/daughter relationship is such that near the conclusion of an episode where Blanche had considered adopting a baby left at their house (long story, Rose was involved) she calls Janet just to "chat." We're not privy to Janet's responses to her mother but can infer from Blanche's words that they are not positive ones and it would seem that Janet was even perplexed as to why her mother was contacting her.

In another episode centered on Mother's Day the audience waits in semi-anguish with Blanche to see if Janet is going to call her. The phone has rung throughout the day as the ladies reminisced and told stories, yet Blanche notes that she has yet to hear from her daughter and indicates a deep hope that she will even though she doesn't really expect to. When the phone at last rings and Blanche excitedly sighs Janet's name in relief the participating audience probably can't help but be relieved as well.

The relationship between Blanche and Rebecca is maybe not as strained as the one with Janet yet it's not exactly on solid footing either. I should note I mean the relationship between Blanche and the second Rebecca.

The first Rebecca was portrayed as an unhappy, overweight, former model engaged to a verbally abusive creep. Inevitably, Blanche helps Rebecca to see her self worth and by the episode's end the odious fiancee has been kicked to the curb. When we next meet Rebecca she is model thin again and portrayed by a completely different actress. Oddly, Blanche also had two different men playing her father, Big Daddy. I guess it's possible that Blanche was non-plussed that her daughter looked like two different persons - she was used to seeing her loved ones morph beyond recognition.

Second Rebecca's trips to Miami allowed for the development of a new, adult connection with her mother. She challenged Blanche's sensibilities by choosing to be artificially inseminated and was intent on raising the child by herself. Blanche though the modern day (female) Casanova is decidedly "old fashioned" in a number of matters including child rearing and believing that a child needs both a mother and a father.

The back and forth between her and Rebecca as they try to hold onto their bond while having markedly separate views feels like an authentic portrayal of the dynamics between mothers and their kids. That's not to say that all mother-child relationships are strained, rather they all are wrapped in a subconscious (and sometimes conscious) pact whereby we, as the children know that they, the parents, are constantly assessing (judging) our life choices so that they can guide us toward the best outcome (ie. tell us where we went wrong and how we could have avoided that if we had just listened to them in the first place).

It's interesting to note that through the first Rebecca and other overweight characters that appear on the show we see all of the understanding and compassion that is usually reserved for characters who struggle within society (whether due to their sexual orientation, age, or skin color) completely evaporate.

Apparently the writer's of the show had no tolerance for people who had weight issues. This is evident from the fat jokes that are lampooned at Rebecca using Sophia as the primary mouthpiece. The horrid fiancee mocks Rebecca for her weight as well, but you're supposed to expect it from him because he's a louse. However, when Sophia is harsh to the girl it's supposed to be funny and Sophia forgiven because she had a stroke and can't control her inner monologue.

Both seem like perfect excuses to pick on the obese. When Sophia meets Rebecca she says to her, "You're Blanche's daughter, the model?" Before turning to Dorothy and Rose to mutter, "What'd she model, car covers?" Given Sophia's progressive views on equality and race relations one would expect her to have a similar stance toward those with weight issues. Yet, like all of us, Sophia is the victim of her own biases: a truth most evident when it comes to her son, Phil.

Like Vera on *Cheers* or Maris on *Frasier*, Phil Petrillo was one of those characters that you so oft heard about but never got to lay eyes on. Since childhood he had plagued Sophia with his need to dress in women's attire. As an adult he continued to cross-dress, plus he married a woman Sophia detested. Together they had ten children, none of whom graduated high school, and the entire family lived in a trailer. Phil was completely misunderstood by his mother who blamed herself for his being "different":

> Rose Nylund: [about Phil] So what if he was different? It's okay that you loved him.
>
> Sophia Petrillo: [voice cracking] I did love him. He was my son, my little boy. But every time I saw him I wondered what I did, what I said, when was the day I did whatever I did to make him the way he was.
>
> Angela Petrillo: [tenderly] What he was, Sophia, was a good man.

Sophia frequently cracked jokes about Phil. Maybe it was to assuage her own discomfort with him and how he chose to live. His wife, Angela, however, loved him for who he was and when he passes away suddenly in season six she goes head to head with Sophia to ensure that Phil's memory isn't tarnished by his mother's inability to understand him.

Dorothy seems more comfortable with her brother's cross-dressing (though she appears somewhat unnerved by Phil being buried in a black teddy), even reminiscing during her eulogy for him that her favorite childhood memories included she and him dressing up like the Bronte sisters. I'm not sure why Phil was buried in Florida when he was always mentioned as having lived in New York. Nor am I sure why none of his ten kids nor his sister Gloria were there for the funeral.

Come to think of it, in an episode from season one when Dorothy tells Sophia not to argue with Phil's wife when she goes to Brooklyn for a visit Sophia replies,

"We get along okay. Phil's wife has her good points. She's sweet, she's reliable, and when her father gets out of prison she'll be a wealthy woman!" I'll just refer us back to the previous aside regarding the two Rebeccas and the two Big Daddy's and leave it at that.

Sophia didn't always understand her son, but she does make the case in multiple episodes that she had affection for him noting, "I love all my children... even Phil."

I wonder if she would have loved Quincy? Following my sister having come home with the arsenal of dog training supplies he became one spoiled pup.

Each night for the first year of his life he was put to bed in his crate after having been regaled with stories of brave canines rescuing princesses and slaying dragons. He was tucked in with a dish towel warmed in the microwave and snored loudly to a playlist of music we made him. He doesn't get a personal stream of lullabies anymore, but he still snores. And, he still smells like corn meal.

* Note: Quincy passed away before this book was published. At twelve years and eight months old we lost him during emergency surgery to remove cancerous tumors. Not a day goes by that I don't miss him and pretend to hear him snoring near by.

Bias

"She happens to like girls instead of guys. Some people like cats instead of dogs. Frankly, I'd rather live with a lesbian than a cat. Unless the lesbian sheds, then I don't know." - Sophia

---

The other day a student asked me if it was possible that her grandson who is gay "became that way" because she watched women's gymnastics with him when he was a kid. I asked her to clarify. She then said, "I used to watch gymnastics with him when he was a kid, did that turn him gay?" I honestly didn't know how to respond without slapping her silly so I took a deep breath, quickly prayed for patience, and then explained biology to her.

Given the plethora of information and scientific inquiry that is available to everyone it is hard to believe that in our day and age there are those who still believe that a gay person can be "turned" gay.

It's possible that due to their own ignorance or lack of information they fail to understand the lack of choice inherent for gay people. They might also not really understand or maybe they ignore the hardships and discrimination that face LGBTQ people even today.

If we choose to believe that being gay or lesbian, transgender, bisexual, or queer is a choice then we also have to buy in to the idea that they these same people are gluttons for punishment. Nobody would purposefully *choose* to be discriminated against, shunned by other members of society, ridiculed, belittled, and bullied. Nobody in their right mind is going to *choose* to live a life where they are thought of as an aberration.

People *have* chosen to join Nazi's and neo-Nazi's. People have chosen to drop atomic bombs. People have chosen to wipe out beautiful species of animals from the face of the earth. People choose to be biased, ignorant, and cruel. The hunters who wiped out the native Buffalo weren't imprisoned for their actions but the wonderful playwright Oscar Wilde was because he loved men. Alan Turing helped the Allies to win World War II. His reward? He was outed as a homosexual and chemically castrated. He later took his own life.

What does it say about the human condition that many Nazi's who took part in the Holocaust weren't imprisoned or hung for their crimes but throughout history up to the present people are imprisoned for who they love? An uncle of mine used to always say to us kids (and it's possible he stole it from Rodney King's televised plea for an end to the '92 LA Riots), "Can't we all just get along?" Or more simply put by Sophia Petrillo, "Everyone wants someone to grow old with and shouldn't everyone have that chance?"

When put in such simple terms the desire to be loved and have a significant other should be universally understood and accepted. Yet bias continues in this world whether it be toward people's sexual preferences, the color of their skin, their religion (or lack thereof), and any other of a multitude of baseless reasons.

Even the GG's had prejudices and biases that they had to contend with through the course of the show. The fact that these amazing characters were shown as being incredibly strong and yet also capable of human depravity is perhaps what allows for the show's influence and popularity to continue to thrive.

Dorothy's son wanted to marry an older black woman. Dorothy didn't oppose because the bride-to-be was black but rather because she was a lot older (of course if we delve into continuity and the show's own lack of comprehensiveness we would remember that her son should actually be in his forties thus making his bride's age a moot point).

Rose's daughter slept with Dorothy's son and because Michael, Dorothy's son, was a musician and not college bound like her daughter, Rose felt he was beneath her child.

Of the four main characters, Sophia was perhaps the most self-actualized, whereas Blanche was the complete opposite. The one issue that probably plagued Blanche the most? Her misunderstanding of and bias toward homosexuality (and that's not counting her confusing lesbians with the Lebanese).

Oblivious to her biases Blanche is forced to deal with them when her younger brother Clayton comes out to her and her roommates as homosexual. Somewhat unaware that her prejudices were in fact prejudices when faced with them, Blanche is almost shocked to find that her friends think that she isn't as tolerant and hip as she thinks she is.

Blanche is instantly confused about her brother when he comes out to her. She points out to him that he had always been a "ladies man" as she falsely believed that he had chased as many skirts through the years as she had slacks. Upon being told by her brother that he had been feigning his interest in women in order to fit in, Blanche is dumbfounded and willfully refuses to believe it.

It's not with malicious intent that she refuses to believe her brother is gay, but rather a deep rooted ignorance and a desperate need to "keep up appearances."

Having never had to walk a mile in Clayton's shoes his societal choices such as getting married to a woman seem to prove to Blanche that Clayton is wrong about his sexuality. She can't quite reconcile the Clayton who had hid part of himself from her all those years with the one who was standing before her asking for her acceptance.

On the one hand, this naivity on her part is sweet for she believes everyone is like her - what you see is what you get. She does not seem to grasp that many people go through life having to hide their true selves.

On the other hand, this level of willful ignorance is indicative of her own latent prejudices. In an episode hilariously titled, *Wham, Bam, Thank You Mammy*, Blanche is faced with the fact that her father had had a torrid love affair with her African-American nanny. At that revelation she was not shocked that her father carried on with her non-white caregiver. Rather she was angry that said nanny had abandoned her as a child (this was because Mammy and Big Daddy had been found out by Big Mommy and Mammy had to make a run for it before Big Mommy got out Big Shotgun).

By the end of the episode with Clayton, Blanche finds herself wanting to be there for her brother and actively choosing to love him for who he is rather than ostracize him for not being who she wants. Well, sort of.

Two years later she receives a letter from Clayton saying that he has big news to share with her about which she says; "I bet I know what the surprise is... Clayton's met himself a girl, and he wants me to meet her." Dorothy chastises her and reminds her that Clayton is gay to which she responds, "Dorothy, I think that gay thing was just a phase he was going through."

Upon Clayton's arrival with his fiancee, Doug, we, the audience, are privy to how nonsensical Blanche can be (and Rose is the dumb one?) when she says to her friends: "I don't really mind Clayton being homosexual, I just don't like him dating men...there must be homosexuals who date women?" Sophia explains to her that there are; "They're called lesbians."

Why do we feel we have an entitlement as to how or who somebody else loves? That has always perplexed me. The fact that there had to be a fight; a long emotionally fraught struggle for LGBTQ people to have the right to get married is baffling. Who has the time and emotional wherewithal that it takes to go out of their way to prohibit another person from being who they are or living how they want? I don't have the energy most days to get out of my pajamas let alone lead a crusade to prohibit a faction of the population from expressing their love.

Maybe that's just it - maybe it's that some of us think we know what's best for all of us and that continues to fuel the bigotry still thriving in the world today. Our inability to accept others differences is perhaps more of a reflection of our own failure to break from the herd than it is a rejection of their failure to assimilate. Or maybe, like Blanche, it also has something to do with appearances.

Typical of Blanche's reaction to, or rather her overreaction to things, she admonishes Clayton for wanting to marry Doug. She tries to persuade him to realize what people will think of *her* should *he* marry a man.

It is often that way for Blanche - she has an ongoing obsession with what others may think of her based on the actions of someone else entirely.

She's okay with her own reputation as a wanton slut, she's quite proud of that. However, when Rebecca (the slim curly haired Rebecca not the chubby straight haired one) wants to have a baby by artificial insemination Blanche's feelings toward her daughter's choice stem from what others might think about her (Blanche) having a daughter who is the unwed mother of a test-tube baby.

Ever the narcissist, she fails to take into account that it's simply not about her, it's about the other person and who they are or what they want for *their* lives. Perhaps this is the great failing of humans - we spend more time worried about what others might think about us and our loved ones that we don't use our heads.

We care so much for the opinions of strangers that we fail our children, our parents, our lovers, and friends by not considering how they feel, what their experience is, what validation they might need in their life at that moment. If we could but remember that nobody outside of our circle of loved ones is really thinking about us at all then the lives of the ones we love could be easier for they would be recipients of our love and support and not a heart broken by our own selfishness.

Letting Go

"…let me get this straight. We lived with a filthy pig in our house, bought a whole bunch of stuff on credit we can't afford, and now we're gonna kiss off 100,000 bucks because the pig is homesick? Sometimes life really bites the big one."
- Sophia

Following the unexpected death of her husband Blanche made a point of putting up barriers in relationships. She couldn't take herself out of the dating pool, her libido was too prolific for that. However, when faced with matters of the heart she struggled to be vulnerable. George's death left her with a heart break that she was adamant not to experience again.

Rose, on the other hand fell for the college professor, Miles, and enjoyed the pleasures that come from an intimate relationship. Yet, Rose did struggle at times with the idea of fully giving herself to the new relationship. Over the course of several episodes throughout the series' run each woman battled with the idea of letting go and moving forward. "Letting go" in particular came up often and proved time and again to be something of a struggle for each of the women.

It probably goes without saying that the concept of letting go (or moving forward) is different for everyone. For my extremely uptight and incapable of relaxing English husband he gets twisted into balls of frustration and anxiety when he needs to move on and put something behind him. It is as though he is nearly physically incapable of allowing himself to be free.

He asked me once, "Dear, how would one go about the letting go of something if they were so inclined?" I thought it over and then told him, "You just do." He blinked at me from across the table with a look that seemed to convey that he was not impressed with my answer. Still, he trudged on: "Sure, but HOW do you let it go?" I knew the man really needed an answer and I didn't want to let him down. I dug really deep into the confines of my mind for an eloquent answer: "You make the conscious choice to not let the matter affect you anymore." He told me I was fired.

Later that week on the *Big Bang Theory* Sheldon was also having a difficult time with letting something go. Penny helped by advising him to imagine his problem as a pen and then to essentially drop the pen as a symbolic letting go (naturally there was more to it than this since Sheldon was involved, but that's a different story). The Brit paused the t.v. as we watched this scene, turned to me and said, "Why didn't *you* explain it like *that?*" Insert exasperated deep sigh from me here.

In a sad, yet bittersweet and poignant episode of the *Girls* Blanche's brother-in-law, Jamie Devereaux, comes to Miami. He and Blanche paint the town together. Over the course of several days the two enjoy Miami as well as a light hearted easiness within their relationship which for her, seems to ignite romantic feelings.

Believing that she's falling in love with him, Blanche embarrasses herself by professing feelings for Jamie who doesn't feel the same. Jamie realized she didn't love him but rather it was her old feelings for George being projected on to him. Kindly, he told her, "You're in love with the memory of George I've brought back to you." Heart broken at the truth, Blanche concedes before locking herself in her room to yet again mourn her lost love.

Marital relationships frequently appear as a theme throughout the show. For Dorothy and Stan the lesson was usually about forgiveness, yet in *Stan Take a Wife* (from season four) Dorothy finds herself in the awkward position of having to let Stan go.

Given his history of being a schmuck it should be easy for Dorothy to fork him over to his intended, Katherine. However, prior to his nuptials, Stan uses force in a stand off at the hospital over Sophia's well being. This act of aggression and chivalry from Stan reminds Dorothy of those times in their marriage when he wasn't causing her grief or hurt but rather made her proud. Subsequently, she makes the decision to stop his marriage to Katherine so that she might be with him again.

Luckily for Dorothy (and Katherine) she revealed her intentions to her friends leading Blanche and Rose to thwart her schemes. In the end, Dorothy has an anonymous encounter with Katherine (in the bar of the hotel where the wedding is taking place) and discovers a lovely woman who earnestly loves Stan.

Meeting Katherine illustrates for Dorothy the folly in her want of Stan and she capitulates having to let go not only of the idea of being with him again, but also of Stan the person. Ultimately, the marriage to Katherine doesn't work out and Dorothy once again finds herself to be the main woman in Stan's life which at that point was much to her own chagrin.

Letting go is something we all probably feel should

be inherently easy, yet most of us find it to be incredibly cumbersome. The Brit is so bad at letting things go that I saved the song *Let it Go* from *Frozen* onto my phone so as to play it at him each time he spirals on some psychotic rant. These rants are usually ones I've heard before about some problem that is virtually non-existent. Thus, it's easier to hit play on the phone than listen to that particular broken record.

You might think I'm a terrible wife who isn't meeting my spouses' needs. You don't understand how underwhelming his problems usually are. For example: a recent repetitive issue of his was lack of space at work. For an entire summer there were endless ravings about his department being unappreciated in the company and how were they expected to work with no space for their computers, printers, chords, what-have-you.

Mind you, he had his own office, but he had taken up most of space by putting his desk square in the middle of the area. This was because he didn't want to have his back to the door or the window. He does this wherever he has a desk (including at home) as he has an innate need to not be taken by surprise in the event of a zombie apocalypse.

For him the zombie apocalypse is not a question of if it will happen, it's a matter of when. Never-mind that I have continued to point out that zombies make no sense. I mean, if they're dead and essentially existing on what could be deemed basic instinct then they don't actually need to eat. They can't starve to death, they're dead! And, as I pointed out once (or maybe twenty times) that cannibalism is preposterous given that there would a replenishment of wild animals without humans to interfere in their existence thus there would be plenty of meat to be had without resorting to human flesh. I'm not allowed to watch the Walking Dead with him anymore.

Anyway, a few years ago, "space" or lack thereof, continued to be the bane of his work existence. His department actually had offices and an entire room for materials related to their job activities. Yet, he was imminently close to quitting said job upon having to suffer a humiliation that can only be described as inane.

In an attempt to create space the Brit and a co-worker forcibly acquired some cabinets for their stuff by placing said stuff in said cabinets. Naturally, the Brit and company were infuriated when people from the department chose not to fight with them but instead just moved their stuff and let the cabinets go. Yeah, I'm not making this up.

So it's not that I'm a mean wife, it's that I'm a long suffering one who for three months was plagued by the "space rant" of a nutter. In the end his company got his department new, BIGGER offices and he was finally happy. Two weeks later he started working remotely from home. I'm imagining a pen....

Forgiveness

"People waste their time pondering whether a glass is half empty or half full. Me, I just drink whatever's in the glass."
-Sophia

I n the fifth season of the *The Golden Girls'* seven year run Blanche Devereaux (played so superbly by Rue McClanahan) finds out that her beloved dead husband George sired a son with another woman.

Not only did George spawn this son, but said son showed up on her doorstep years after George's untimely death (in a car accident) wanting to know about his father. As any red blooded woman would be, she was outraged.

Having spent years living with fond memories of the only man to whom she was faithful (as you may know, for Blanche that was a big deal) she was suddenly left with a blemished image of him and more importantly with questions to which she could never have the answer: Why or how could he do such a thing? Was it serious or a fling? Did he know she turned down sleeping with Andy Rooney while they were married?

Her friends, ever the comfort in times of grief, came to her aid with pearls of wisdom. Dorothy offerred Blanche two distinct theories as to why men cheat: one is that men are as she says, "Victims of the evolutionary process which genetically programs their sexual habits." The second theory per Dorothy, is that, "Men are scum."

Sophia's sage words of advise were to speak of a time when her Sal nearly cheated on her with a "mouthy bird of a thing," while she was pregnant with her son Phil and "crying all the time."

Rose urged Blanche to look beyond George's actions and forgive him saying, "Don't throw away all the good memories just because of a mistake."

Forgiveness is a major theme throughout the show's run, second in importance only to friendship. In countless episodes one or more of the main characters come to a point where they need to seek the forgiveness of another person.

In many instances Rose, Dorothy, and Blanche find themselves hat in hand with each other over some sort of row or slight. Dorothy and Blanche read Rose's diary. Rose forgave them. Blanche was mad that Rose allegedly slept with Blanche's brother (she didn't). Rose forgave her. Dorothy kisses Miles, Rose's steady beau of the last two seasons of the show. Rose forgave her. Sophia lied to Dorothy when she was a teenager about her prom date ditching her. Dorothy forgave her.

By and large, more time might have been spent on the characters seeking absolution then eating cheesecake. Seems impossible doesn't it? And yet, it's true. Well, maybe it's true. I didn't actually count how many times they ate cheesecake before comparing it to how many times they had to apologize, but I maintain there was a lot of penance going on. So much so there were even two episodes featuring priests.

What then does it mean for our silver foxes that so much of their stories were tied up in their exoneration and absolution? Perhaps this was to illustrate what horrible and unjust people these characters really were.

Or, maybe it was so that said characters could not just learn and grow, but also show how fallible we as humans truly are. Every mistake, every misplaced step or hurtful remark was part of an education for the rest of us.

Dorothy it seems was most often in the role of the forgiver. This was due in part to her having been married to Stan Zbornak. Long after their divorce, Stan continued to be a major part of Dorothy's life and with his presence inevitably came the need for his apologies.

In the beginning (and by beginning I mean the second episode of the series) Stan returns for the wedding of his and Dorothy's daughter, Kate. With the wounds of the divorce still fresh, Dorothy has a difficult time just having him in the same house let alone anywhere near her or her daughter. More than once her friends had to thwart her from strangling him (this is also a recurrent theme). Yet, by the end of the episode, after she tells him what she thinks of him, she begins to forgive him.

A testament to Dorothy's ability as a mother, she doesn't let her feelings toward him stop her from relaying a heartfelt message about the goodness of marriage to her daughter. Though Stan cheated and abandoned her, when Kate suffers from pre-wedding jitters her mother assures her that being married was in fact something worth while. Side note - later in the series we find out Kate's husband cheats on her too. But, as Sophia would say, that's a different story.

Repeatedly, we find Dorothy and Stan engaged in a battle for her forgiveness of him. She also sleeps with him - a lot. That probably doesn't do much to help her confused feelings toward him. These two characters were perpetually locked in what can only be deemed a stalemate: he screws up and after reading him the riot act, she forgives him.

Maybe the Zbornaks work as a metaphor for marriage or all relationships between two people by embodying the give and take that comes with sharing your life with another. We can't all be saints all of the time and when we fail or fall it's usually the person or persons to whom we're closest that suffer the consequences with us. I don't know if it's an innate human need to make those who love us proud or to somehow be worthy of love, but most of us do keep trying to do and be better. We stumble, we get up, we fight on and the one thing that can mean the most when we do make a mess of things is the forgiveness and understanding of our loved ones.

Without forgiveness what does life mean? It would instead be an existence whereby we pitfall into the mire of human depravity. Without someone who means something to us to care that we've fell on our face, for whom would we be trying to improve? Let's face it, each of us left to our devices has little motivation to do or be good. Like the old adage says: if a dog craps on the sidewalk and there is nobody there to scoop it up how many people walk through it and get it on their good shoes? The moral to the story of course being that we're all the pooping dog and the rest of the world is the shoes - so without someone caring enough to help clean up our messes through their love and compassion then essentially we just continuously crap on everybody else.

Therefore, Blanche makes the decision to follow Rose's advice and forgive George. Forgot about that, didn't you? Anyway, beyond forgiving George, Blanche invites the illegitimate son, David, into her home and shares pictures and stories of George with the young man. She chose to exonerate George of his sin against her. Now, I'm not advocating that we all forgive adulterous husbands (or wives), that's something I'm sure has to be on a case-by-case basis. I'm just saying that forgiveness can be a good thing.

As Dorothy can attest, divorce and cheating spouses are really hard on the ego. Blanche's ego wasn't unscathed by the revelation of George's infidelity, that's a hurt she would always have going forward. Yet, she chose to forgive him not for his benefit, but for her own. That and given the show aired in the pre-DVR era many of their back stories (heck, even their names) were changed and retconned indiscriminately depending on any one episode's particular story needs. So, it was only a matter of time before David was changed for a daughter, George was still alive, and Blanche hailed from Cabot Cove, Maine, not Atlanta.

Friendship

Blanche: I also happen to have a room for rent, and the name is Blanche Devereaux.

Rose: Why would you name a room Blanche Devereaux?

I read once something along the lines of, "Friendship is the crazy in you recognizing the crazy in someone else and then saying to that person let's hang out together and share our crazy." It's entirely possible I'm not paraphrasing that correctly. It's even more possible that I'm making the whole quote up. Either way, the gist is: friends are awesome. Unlike our family, we choose our friends so if they suck, that's really more on us than on them.

For the *Golden Girls* the benefit of picking your friends was that they were able to surround themselves with people who were encouraging, uplifting, supportive, and a host of other things that make the daily grind more bearable. Yet the show makes clear that friendship is something that has to be nurtured and grown and doesn't always come naturally.

In the episode "The Way We Met" the audience is shown that the ladies not only didn't immediately hit it off, they truly kind of loathe each other at first. Their differences and constant bickering lead all of them to the conclusion that there were more harmonious people with whom they can live.

Each of them had one foot out the door when Rose

decided to tell a story about a circus of herrings. Yes, it is as ridiculous as it sounds. Yet, the story and some cheesecake provided the ladies with a shared comfort. They attained a sense of ease based on mutual merriment which in turn allowed for them to see that they not only could get along but that it was possible for each of them to thrive in the presence of the other two.

Over the years the cultivation of the friendship among the ladies as well as the addition of the cantankerous Sophia is shown to be hard work. However, this theme of friendship is one that either consciously or not works well with the idea of forgiveness. For the ladies their friendship is underlined by their ability to forgive one another which is a moral code we all could do well to live by I'm sure.

In the episode, "Hey Look Me Over!" a mistake in photo development leads Rose to believe that Blanche slept with Charlie - Rose's now deceased husband.

The supposed indiscretion would have been years prior when Charlie was on a business trip to Miami, but that doesn't make the pain any less present for poor Rose. Obviously, she is crushed to think that Charlie cheated on her (please see the previous chapter on men being scum), but, what makes it more devastating is that it happened with her friend.

Naturally, Rose runs the gamut of emotions but in the end finds that forgiving Blanche is the only way to move forward given that her friend is there and Charlie is not. Of course prior to Rose coming to terms with it all nobody thought to look at *all* of the photos in the pack. Upon doing so Dorothy finds all of the photographs were double exposed thus proving

Blanche innocent of sleeping Charlie but guilty of taking boudoir photographs of herself.

I can say honestly and proudly that I've never cheated on a friend in a photograph of her husband. This is partly because of my moral code and partly because we don't use real film in cameras anymore. Not to mention - who has the energy to primp and take dirty pics of themselves? There is way too much t.v. to be watched to be fiddling around with the camera. Also - I'm pretty sure the Brit would find it more hilarious than sexy. Hell, I'd probably find it more hilarious than sexy. But I digress…

Like the GG's I try to maintain healthy friendships with those ladies who I know I can rely on day or night. I want to say I work at my friendships like the GG's do, but in all honesty I'm not sure that's true. Sometimes I think you've been friends with someone so long that being friends is almost like a habit. It something you do because it's something you enjoy that you've always done.

The good thing about friends as opposed to other habits is that most of the time you don't have to quit your friends like you do with something like smoking. I'm not gonna lie - I loved smoking. Some love drinking, some drugs, and others promiscuous sex with strangers (I was a fan of that too, but I brought my cigarettes with me to the party). For me, the vice du jour was smoking. I loved everything about it. The chronic need to have it in my hand at all times as something to do or have. The taste of the smoke as you inhaled right before it turned to regret and bitterness. The feeling in your chest as it went down your esophagus that probably wasn't something you were actually feeling given that you had charred your lungs from said smoking several decades prior and now like a bad relationship were going through the motions because you didn't know how to break up with the toxic little suckers that are ruining your life and driving away everyone who loved you…. Where was I? Friends! Right…

So, I try to maintain healthy friendships with those ladies who I know I can rely on for ANYTHING. You know the type; the kind of friend who is so loyal that if you call them at four in the morning and advise that you are outside of their house in a van (or truck) with a bag of lye (or bottle of bleach), a shovel (or backhoe), and the tied up body of your dead husband (I'm not really sure why the husband is tied up in this scenario as in all likelihood I would probably have taken him by surprise in a sudden killing with something like the wok or frying pan because I just couldn't listen to him tell me how to load the dishwasher "properly" ONE MORE TIME!) they would go with you out to the desert to bury him no questions asked.

They probably wouldn't help dig, but damn it, they'd hold the flashlight. And, after the grave is filled in you guys would swing into the nearest gas station for a forty of beer and a pack of cigarettes. You would open them then and there in the parking lot under the neon sign that a blinking "s" at the end of the word gas and before silently drinking and puffing in the dark one of you, probably your companion, breaks the silence with a deep sigh and the question, "Dishwasher again?"

At present I have several such friends in my life and of course the no-questions asked desert burial works both ways. I think I might also have this arrangement with a good friend's husband. He's a mumbling low talker and I'm a deaf nodder so when we're together he says things and I pretend to hear them usually by smiling and nodding along.

I have warned his wife that if the day comes that he arrives on my porch with a vehicle dripping blood and shovel in hand that I'm sorry, but I must have nodded in agreement at some point.

Aging

Rose: Wow, Sophia, that was some story!

Sophia: Yeah-funny, touching, and with a surprise twist ending. I wonder if was true. Damn that stroke.

My mother always says that she doesn't mind her birthdays because, "It's better than the alternative." The implication being that the alternative is death (for me, the preferred alternative would be staying at one really good age (like 35) and not getting older). Ergo, she finds that growing older is better than being dead. I'm sure she has a point in there somewhere, but I'm willfully ignoring it. Sure, death is definite and all, but so is aging. Once you're forty you can never be thirty again and my forty year old knees really miss the ones I had back then.

As fans of the *Golden Girls* may know, the Blanche had the most trouble with the idea of aging. Ever confident in her own good looks and youthfulness she still struggled with the ongoing mental battle many of us wage against getting older. Not one to shy away from grabbing the bull by the horns, Blanche was even willing to undergo surgery to get the upper-hand.

In one episode Blanche has a particularly scarring time at a reunion and came home resolved to have a face lift. In another, she decides to have her breasts augmented as (and I'm paraphrasing her here) "big bosoms are fashionable again." In the end she winds up doing neither of those things and instead of having the "boob job" she donates the money she was going to use so that Sophia's aging friend may live in a nicer retirement home where she'll receive better care for her Alzheimer's disease.

What then does it mean for the rest of us when a woman as vain as Blanche forgoes cosmetic enhancements? Is aging a state of mind or a state of appearance? If it's the former, I'm screwed: my current state of mind is that I'm a forty year old white woman trapped in the body of a ninety year old Sumo wrestler who gave up the job but not the food.

If we agree that aging is a state of mind nobody aged better than Sophia Petrillo. Throughout the series that woman cooked, she travelled (including a quick turnaround to Sicily to make amends with a spurned lover), she volunteered at the hospital, and frequented her local Senior Center. She was a woman who wasn't afraid of dying so much as she was determined to live her life with gusto. It would be baffling to Sophia to not "rage against the dying light" as Dylan Thomas suggested in his poem *Do Not Go Gentle Into that Good Night*. On more than one occasion she tried to help others follow her lead in accepting that aging wasn't a state of mind or looks but rather it was a state of doing and being.

In a classic episode titled *Not Another Monday*, Sophia's friend, Martha, is tired of waiting for death and old age to come get her. Rather than dying slowly and painfully from any of an assortment of ailments she didn't yet have she decided to put an end to things in advance.

Personally, I can't slight Martha for wanting to jump

off the train early. I have repeated time and again to my sister and husband: if ever I get terminally ill or something really debilitating then one day you'll probably just find me, dead, with a Post-It note stuck to one hand that reads, "I'm over it." Like Martha told Sophia, "I feel that I don't have the courage to die by inches." Although, does anybody? Do we face dying bravely or is more of a resignation?

In 2016 (the year the music not only died, but it died a gruesome death, was pissed on by a hobo and then lit on fire before its remains were swept up and tossed in a urinal) when the shocking news came out that David Bowie (God) had died. The media reported that he had been sick with cancer for eighteen months. Yet, two days before his death (and on his birthday no less) he "dropped" a final album. Prior to that he had even filmed a video for the single *Lazarus* among a slew of other feats including overseeing the creation of a Broadway play also titled Lazarus. At some point near the end of those eighteen months Bowie had to know that the end was nigh.

I can't help but think that he didn't bother with the notion of being brave in the face of death, there was too much left to do before he ran out of time. Recording an album while in the midst of his own demise feels as though Bowie didn't just rage against the aforementioned light: he grabbed it, used it to light a smoke, and then smashed it with his bare hands. Thus, if life is for living then maybe death is even more so.

I love the notion that upon death each person who has grabbed life by the gusto and made the most of it can skip the reflections and admonishing and just be at peace knowing that they had truly lived. Living of course is in and of itself different for each person. For many, living is a freedom found in spending time with family and friends. I'm not sure that it has to be complicated by what we as individuals have done or whether or not we've been successful, how much money we've amassed, and if we're leaving behind some kind of lasting legacy.

Legacy's themselves are a funny thing. There are very few Einstein's, Shakespeare's, and Elvis Presley's in the annals of the world's history. Instead there are lots of mothers, friends, sons and daughters: nameless and unknown to those whose path theirs didn't cross. But, for those they did these people were maybe loving, trusting, funny, or wise companions. They were the person on whom someone else counted and truly isn't that the lasting legacy?

So, what then of Sophia's friend Martha? She died. Well, I'm assuming at some point she died, however, in the episode in question Sophia talked her out of it by promising to be there for her "like a best friend." I wonder if Martha thanked Sophia for being a friend... for traveling down the road and back again? I could go on, but it's already in your head thus my work here is done.

ABOUT THE AUTHOR

T.A. Pryor resides in California (not the good bit of the state, the armpit of the state) with her husband, the Brit. Together they have too many cats, two turtles, and a partridge in a pear tree. When she's not writing or teaching the author is sleeping, eating, avoiding being productive, working a crossword, or playing Disney's Emoji Blitz because it's crazy addictive and she just can't put it down. Stupid game.

30682933R00040

Made in the USA
Middletown, DE
26 December 2018